Balancing Your Blended Family

Practical Tips and Insight to Help
Your Blended Family Work!

I0151937

Jason D. King

Please note that the name "satan" is purposefully not capitalized in this book.

Published by

Jason D. King

P.O. Box 3147

Summerville, SC 29484

Order online at

<u>wordofdeliverancecc.org</u>

Balancing Your Blended Family

Dedication

To my loving and supportive wife Rhonda and our children Jasmyne, Cameron, Christopher and Jaiden. Words cannot fully express the love I have for my family. Thank you for allowing me the honor of taking care of you. We are unbreakable.

To my mother Lola King and my father Keith McFadden. Thank you for preparing me to be the man that I am today.

To God. Thank you for your faithfulness and for bringing the vision to pass.

CONTENTS

Introduction

What is a blended family? A blended family is a family where one or both members of the couple have children from a previous relationship. Statistics suggest that blended families are the predominant family in the United States today. Two factors contribute to this. The first is fornication, or sex outside of marriage. Our society has left the wholesome values of the Bible to become an increasingly hedonistic people. We want sex and lots of it. We've gone about this the wrong way. The Bible instructs us that sex should only be between a husband and wife. Yes, sex should be between two people in a covenant commitment. Long gone are the values of television's Huxtables and Cleavers. The entertainment industry glorifies meaningless hookups but rarely, if ever, show the consequences. Constant exposure to this message of casual sex enflames lust in people. This gets played out in non-covenant relationships in which children are the by-products. Some of us then choose to marry, but we can't leave our children behind and start over. When we get married, our children are grafted into the new family unit.

The second factor is divorce and remarriage. Statistics show that almost half of all marriages end in divorce. When someone remarries the children come along for the journey. It would be easier if both parents stayed single, but that isn't how the scenario typically plays out. Mom and Dad want to love again and usually find someone else to share their life with. Sharing a life includes sharing the responsibilities of children before this new marriage.

How do I balance and bring order to all the issues that confront my blended family? An overwhelming majority of new blended family parents don't know where to get help for their marriage, children, stepchildren and new blended family. This is my purpose for writing this book. I want to help you! I want to give you practical tips and insight to help your blended family work. This book will answer the questions you have and the questions you didn't know you needed to ask. It is my prayer that you will gain peace and order in your home by using this book as a guideline for balancing your blended family.

1

"I MET A WOMAN"

One word could sum up where I was in my life—tired. I was surrounded by the same people and doing the same things that didn't give me the life I thirsted for. The nightlife, the women, the alcohol and the games had lost their luster. There was a void in my life, a yearning to be fulfilled that couldn't be met. I did not confess to be a Christian, but I was brought up with a consciousness of God. My mother taught me to pray. She was a strong woman who insisted on instilling the fear of God into her children. This usually worked to her benefit. We were threatened by her telling God on us all the time. If we did anything wrong, she would say, "I'll just send up a prayer." We all had the same fear. "No, Mama, please don't tell God on us." Then she would say, "All right now, y'all better listen." As a single woman bringing up four boys and a girl, she probably had to use this scare tactic. There were some New Year's Eves that we didn't make it to church. I can remember her saying, "All right, get down on your knees. It's almost 12 o'clock." We would kneel on the floor with our hands together and eyes reverently closed and begin to pray. We had moved a few times, and the floors were vinyl, carpet or wood. No matter the surface, our knees always found their way to the floor. Yes, we did attend a Pentecostal church, Christ Church Cathedral. Bishop B.E. Sharper, my mother's uncle, was the pastor, but we didn't go all the time. The one thing that I do remember was how constant those New Years Eve prayers were. They taught me reverence for God and the knowledge that I could talk to Him. I went to live with my father during my sophomore year in high school. His mother, my grandmother, was a Baptist preacher, and my father and his siblings were in church all their adolescent years. When I went to live with him, he didn't attend church, but guess what? I had to go. To this day, I am grateful that he made me go. I began to attend my grandmother's church, Canaan Missionary Baptist Church, where the Reverend Dr. Alfred Williams was the pastor. I was saved and baptized there but soon fell away from being a disciplined Christian. This, however, didn't stop me from attending as an adult. No matter what time I got in on Sunday morning , I would set my alarm to get up and catch the service at least two Sundays each month. I guess I am a living example of Proverbs 22:6, "Train up a child the way he should go: and when he is old, he will not depart from it."

Armed with this God-consciousness, I made a decision. I didn't want to keep doing the same things and continue being in unfulfilling relationships. I remember being in the nightclub and saying to myself, "This is boring." The bright lights were dimming the music was halting, and the lust was losing its pull on me. The smokescreen that satan had on my mind was drifting away. At this pivotal point in my life, I said, "There has got to be more to life than this." That might have been the only time I left the party before it ended. I was lonely. I wanted companionship, not just meaningless dates. I remember one night I couldn't get any of my usual female friends to go out with me. Most had dates with their boyfriends. I know, that sounds really bad. I wanted someone to call my own. Living in my sin and still armed with a God-consciousness instilled in childhood, I prayed. "Lord, I'm tired of this lifestyle. Send me a good woman. Send someone who loves You and would love me, too." I was praying out of frustration. I had some audacity. I was living like a first-class sinner but had the nerve to call on the Holy One of Israel. In spite of me, the merciful and gracious God of all creation answered my prayers.

I met Rhonda through a mutual friend. I had been talking to him about making a change in my life. He told Rhonda about me and me about her. One day, I decided to go by his workplace to talk to him. A young lady met me, and I asked her if she knew my friend. She was very helpful and got him for me. He came around the corner smiling and grinning and talked to both of us. Later that night, he called to ask what I thought. About what, I asked? "About Rhonda. She's the one I was telling you about," he said. Rhonda had been working on her relationship with God and wasn't really looking to be in a relationship. She had been in bad relationships, and meeting new people wasn't on her priority list. With a little convincing from my friend, though, she went on a double date with us with a understanding that it was only a "friend date." She didn't want me to expect anything more than good, clean fun. We had dinner and shot pool. The night was filled with laughs and great conversation. We had a great time on our first friend date and then had one more. When I suggested we go out by ourselves, just the two of us, she agreed. Talking to her was refreshing. It wasn't the same, tired conversation that always got around to sex. We talked about God, current events, politics, family and whatever the day had brought. She was interested in me and not in what I had or what I could do for her. We talked for hours, and the conversation often ended up with one of us asking, "Did you fall asleep?" I wanted to know about her and what made her be the woman she was. I was there when she needed me. I could tell that life hadn't been easy for her, so anything I could do to make her smile made me happy. I was gaining her trust. That wall of protection she had erected was crumbling. We were building a relationship. For the first time, I talked to my roommate about a woman I met and didn't mention physical attraction. This surprised both of us. We were young, hardworking men who took advantage of all sin had to offer. But I was changing. I started to attend church services with Rhonda. Because I respected her, I listened to Gospel music in her presence and soon began listening to it when she wasn't around. I was attracted to her spirit and wanted to comfort and protect her. God does hear the prayers of sinners. I met a woman who drew me closer to Him and was falling in love with her.

2

"LIVESTOCK"

Most men are not quick to bring women home to meet their mothers. It could have great potential for disaster. We may feel that we would lose a part of our voice in the relationship once we cross this threshold. What happens if the mother and girlfriend bond? She talks to her now more than you. Then your mom refers to her as the daughter she never had. All of a sudden, they start making plans that include you, without your participation! The next thing you know, you're in church with a ring and a tux hearing those words of commitment, "I do." And you didn't even have a chance to propose.

Then there's the other extreme. What if this woman you're dating connects with your family and you lose a connection from her? Now, when you end the relationship, you have to call a family conference to brief everyone. What if this happens more than once? The whole family struggles to remember the new girlfriend's name, while trying to forget the names of the previous three. At Thanksgiving, two family members called her by the wrong name, and you have to deal with the hurt feelings. Your family likes her, but they loved the previous girl you brought home. Talk about awkward. You don't want to be perceived as a womanizer to your sweet mother and little sister, and surely you don't want to set the wrong example for your brothers. To avoid such complicating scenarios, most men don't bring women home soon into a relationship. Rarely did I mention my relationships to my mother. I felt they would only bring on nosey personal questions that I did not want to be bothered with. I can count the women I've introduced to my mother on one hand with a finger to spare. I just believe that a relationship should have real potential before people start getting all intimate with my family. Rhonda and I were doing well. We enjoyed spending time together and cared deeply for each other. We did the usual movies, bowling, and dinner. I liked and enjoyed her family. They were loving people and easy to talk to. You may ask why I met her family before she met mine. That sounds like a double standard. I met Rhonda's family first because she lived with her mother, and that's where I picked her up for dates. I also think it's proper for a family to know who's taking out their daughter or sister. She is a woman and needs to be protected. We've all heard, "You never know. They could be a murderer or someone crazy." So the more we went out, the more I got to know her family. Her mother was a charming woman who loved everyone. Her father died when she was a teenager, and this strong woman reared three girls by herself. Rhonda had two sisters and an adopted brother. We all came to know each other well. This was a loving family that taught me the agape love of God. They were unselfish, and although they didn't have much, seemed to find a way to give to others. They were and still are loving people. Rhonda had two young children, Jasmyne and Cameron. This was new to me. I was used to being with women with children, but not being in a solid relationship with them. I didn't have any children and had always thought of myself as a hot commodity. I was young, with no children, no arrest record and a history of stable employment. I envisioned meeting a woman with no children and starting a family with her. God had different plans. His thoughts are not ours, and His ways are higher than ours. I respected how Rhonda cared for her children. They were always dressed nice, and you could see that they were priority in her life. She often got them ready for bed before we left to go out and made sure we got back at a decent hour. She never wanted her children to wake up and find her not there. I found this very attractive. I knew women who put men before their children, but not Rhonda.

[Women, a good man is concerned about how you take care of your children. A good man will not be interested in you if your hair, makeup, nails and outfit are flawless, but your children look like they are neglected. That shows that you care about yourself more than your children. The same time and effort you take in grooming yourself should also be taken with your children. Your children are representations of you. When they look bad, you look even worse. When I see this scenario, it shows the selfish nature of that woman. She cares more about herself than that which came out of her womb. If she is a selfish

mother, then surely the possibility is great that she will be a selfish wife. I would tell myself, "I'll pass on that." It does not matter how good she looks, cooks or loves. She is not wife-material for me. Think about this. If a man is okay with your not caring for your children, maybe he won't care for them either. Now you could be setting up an atmosphere for potential abuse and your children's resenting both of you for feeling left out and unloved.]

Maybe I admired Rhonda because she reminded me of how my mother took care of us. We didn't have much, but what we did have was clean and presentable. My mother made sure our needs came before hers. Rhonda presented herself to me as a lady and not an object to be lusted after. She was confident but not arrogant. She was firm but still yielding. I had never felt like this before. This relationship was not about what I could get out of it. I was more concerned about her and her children's well-being than my own. I felt Rhonda and I were going somewhere. I wanted to introduce her to my mother and I did.

I decided to talk to my mother about this woman I met. I wanted to prep her, so I wouldn't be embarrassed or have Rhonda feel uncomfortable when I brought her over. I told my mother about this woman I met and how I loved her. I gave her the highlights of our relationship and told her how happy I was. I mentioned that she had two children. I didn't know what kind of reaction to expect. I had been doing well on my own, and maybe my mother thought this would slow me down. You know how mothers are about their boys. She may have wondered why I willingly entered into a relationship with a woman who had two children. I was nervous about what she might say and braced myself just in case. To my surprise, she said, "Well, son, if you love the cow, you've got to love the calves. As long as ya'll love each other, ya'll be okay." Wow! That was a weight off my shoulders. I was stressing over nothing. That went better than I thought. I brought Rhonda over to meet my family, and everything went well. They liked her and she liked them. We found out that my mother knew a lot of her family and her dad, the Late Great Larry Brown. He was a well known pianist and soloist with a reputation for helping anyone in need. Everybody knew him! Later, we went to meet my father. His reaction was the same. I'm not the type who needs the approval of others to do what I know in my heart is God's will. I do, however, value the opinions and advice of those close to me. My mother and father's approving of our relationship was special to me. Later I thought, why would they not approve? My mother was a single parent of five and could understand wanting someone to love you and your children. She struggled to provide for us and had a few boyfriends, but never a husband to love all of us. My father took care of my brother, who was not his biological son, up until he graduated from high school. How great of a man he was to do this without treating my brother and me differently. I didn't know this until I was an adult. He knows how it is to be moved by compassion and love to bring up a child who isn't biologically yours. I felt love and compassion for Rhonda and the children. I wanted to do anything I could to ease her burden and help them. She was beautiful inside and out, and the love we shared was a gift from God that we couldn't deny each other. As our relationship grew, she allowed me more access to the children. I helped any way I could with them.

[Women, you must be careful how much access your boyfriend has to your children. The relationship should be serious before children are heavily involved. What if it doesn't work out? What if the next relationship doesn't work out? How many partners

will your children see you with? How many unrelated uncles are they going to have. Make sure that the relationship is serious and has good potential before bringing your children into it. They have feelings and make mental observations, and their lives will be affected by the relationship choices you make.]

Okay. We crossed this hurdle. Our families were acquainted and all is well. Rhonda and I are doing great and starting off on good footing.

I was completely surprised by what happened next. I got a phone call from a woman I had been involved with a few months earlier. She said she was in the hospital. I asked what was wrong. She was pregnant. Forgive me for being selfish, but this was how I felt. Imagine a hot air balloon on the ground being filled to capacity. At the moment we are about to take off, the weather changes, and wind and rain batter the balloon from all sides. All of a sudden, a bolt of lightning strikes the balloon which then deflates. I was that deflated balloon. I was in this beautiful relationship. A change in the "weather" threatened to end it as fast as it started. How would I explain this to Rhonda? I didn't want to add to the disappointments she had already faced. Surely, our relationship would be over. I was so caught up in selfishness that I resisted being happy over having a wonderful son who would bring me so much joy. Not only did Rhonda have calves, I had one on the way, too!

3

"MAN UP"

"Man up" is an expression that usually means "get it done "or "take responsibility for it." There is a void in our culture left by men not stepping up to the plate and being responsible. We lie and avoid conflict, instead of being the man God created us to be. I learned this lesson years ago when I lied to my mother about what I was doing one night. I told her I was going one place, but really went to another. This resulted in my license plate being stolen and the filing of a police report. I talked to my uncle about the situation and expressed my desire to keep this from my mother. After I gave him all the scenarios in which I could lie, he said, "Well, you can always tell the truth." Wow! I hadn't thought of that. And many men don't consider the truth to be their first option, either. I was going to lie until the end. That's what most people do. Confronted with a decision, I decided to tell my mother the truth. She confessed that she didn't believe me anyhow. At that point in my life, I found liberation. All I had to do is tell the truth. I would avoid the heavy shackles of having to tell more lies to keep up with the first. The truth is liberating because it requires no maintenance. It stands on its own. I adopted confronting life's issues on that day. I would not run or hide from my responsibilities. I would face them like a man. There is peace in tackling them head on. Okay. So, now I'm telling the truth. I didn't say it was going to be easy.

I was perplexed. How would I break the news to Rhonda? I talked to our mutual friend, the one who introduced us. He shared my concern and assured me she would understand. That was easy for him to say.

He wasn't the one who had to break the news to her. To this day, my friend is still one of the most optimistic people I know.   I was concerned about how Rhonda would feel and how her family would view me. By no means was this simple. We had just started a beautiful relationship, and now another woman is having my son. I knew I wasn't a bad guy, but even I could see the potential for embarrassment and drama that was sure to impact our relationship. I sat on the news for a week. I needed to clear my mind and settle my spirit. Once settled, I could figure out how to tell Rhonda. The truth is that, if you wait for a perfect time to do something like this, you probably never will. I had to man up. I prayed and finally went to Rhonda's house. In her living room, I explained the situation. I let her know this happened before we met and that I was no longer involved with the mother–to- be. I poured out my heart to her and expressed my desire for our relationship not to end. I apologized for any pain and embarrassment I caused her. This was one of the hardest things I had to do in my life. Owning up to disappointing the one you love always is. As I talked, it was like wounding myself. Rhonda's face fell lower and lower. I got it all out, told the truth and expressed my feelings. It was in God's hands. She took a few minutes. It was a lot to process. She took a deep breath, grabbed my hands

and said "Okay, this is what we are going to do...."
What! I thought she was going to kick me out of the
house. In the middle of processing everything, she
had comforted me. She said everything would be all
right and that we would make it through. As I write
this, it still warms my heart. She had a reason to exit
the relationship but chose to stay. How selfless of
her. She didn't have to put up with that, and surely
there was no shortage of men who would want to
date her. I was floored, speechless and grateful. I
had never experienced such unconditional love from a
woman. She put me before herself, and that was new
to me. This woman really taught me how to love, and
I felt God's unconditional love through her. I loved
her more because of how she loved me. From that
moment on, our time together was more than a
relationship. It was romantic destiny that must be
fulfilled.

I had never been to a wedding until I met Rhonda. It
was really not a part of the culture I was exposed to. I
knew a few married people but not many. When two
people were in a relationship, they would just live
together. "Shacking up" is the term the church uses
for it, and it only produces the sin of fornication. I
knew that shacking up wasn't an option and, if we got

serious, marriage was the only way. Her mother and father were married sixteen years before he died. Many of her family members were married. I went to a few weddings with Rhonda, and she was in most of them. To me, it was like she was always the bridesmaid but deserving of being a bride. We continued to date for about a year and a half, and just like any relationship, had our ups and downs. I wanted to spend the rest of my life with Rhonda and hoped that she would feel the same. We had browsed some bridal sets on a previous outing. I paid careful attention to what she liked. I purchased a set and hid it in the closet of my house. I looked at that ring every day until I gave it to her. It was one of the biggest purchases I made outside of my car.

[Men, your wife should not have to hide her wedding ring because of embarrassment. You should do the best of your ability to see that you show your heart in the presentation of the ring that you give her. The Bible tells us that where a man's treasure is, his heart will be also. This means that what you spend money on is what you love. If the rims on your car, shoe collection, flat screen television, video game system, golf clubs or other superficial items cost more than the ring you are looking at, you may want to reconsider that ring. I'm not saying that if you have purchased

an inexpensive ring that you don't love your wife. What I am saying is that we should properly plan and save so that we represent ourselves well on her finger. Just giving her a ring is not enough. We should offer her the best we can. After all, that ring can say a lot to others about you.]

Because Rhonda's father went to be with the Lord, I asked her mother for her blessing. She obliged me, and now I had to plan the moment. We went out on a date for her birthday. We ate at a nice restaurant and concluded our date on the beach. We talked for hours. Even though we were sure of each other, I believe we were conducting final interviews. We talked about our goals and continued to open up to each other. Okay, now I was sure. I got down on one knee and proposed as the sun rose over the Atlantic Ocean. To me, that sun represented newness for both of us, a new day, new chapter, new season and new life together. Six months later, we became husband and wife. I was now the man of the house and responsible for my wife and our three children. Our daughter, Jaiden, would be born four years later. And that's the way we became the Brady Bunch.

That's the beginning of our story.   I wanted to let you in on how our relationship started so that you would understand the heart of the words that follow. I have encountered many challenges with my blended family. I'm sure that you have or will have with yours. We can eliminate a lot of unnecessary stress with the proper guidance. It is my desire to share with you what I've learned through years of counseling to, ministering on, and most of all, living in a blended family. I pray that you find answers and direction to help your marriage survive the challenges of a blended family. The following chapters cover key topics that must be addressed for a blended family to be successful. I pray that you let the Holy Spirit minister to you as you read what God has granted me to share.

4

"TUG OF WAR"

"It's you and me against the world." Rhonda and I use this saying a lot in our marriage. It simply means that we will not let anyone divide us or control how we manage our home. It's important to embrace this principle because many people will try to tell you what you should or should not do in managing your home. The non-custodial parent, your parents, grandparents, siblings, uncles, aunts, school officials, church members, television specials and news articles will all have something to say about this. If you follow all the advice you receive, you won't be mentally stable.   What works for some, may not work for you. I'm not saying that we should be stubborn and ignore wise counsel. I am saying that we must learn to process all information and use what is beneficial to our situation. In spite of what others say, you must do what God is leading you to do. He is the author and finisher of our faith and knows what is best for us. After all, it's your home. You're the responsible party. You and your spouse need to make every effort to barricade it against attacks that will divide you.

(Key point: *A person does not have the right to manage a home he or she does not live in.)*

When receiving counsel, consider the source. Let me put this in perspective. I'm not saying that we should mute the voice of certain groups that give us counsel, but it would be wise to consider their circumstances. If I'm married, I'm more cautious about counsel from those who are single. They may not understand the dynamics of a covenant relationship. If they do, they lack experience. If you had a medical problem, whom would you consult, a physician with twenty years' experience or a pre-med student? I would also be cautious of counsel from those with noticeably bad marriages. Their disappointment could cause them to give you biased information and cloud your decision making. No one's marriage is perfect, but some are worse than others. Those in bad marriages could give advice that has nothing to do with your marriage but everything to do with theirs. Single people will offer their advice, too. Single people have given me more than their two cents' worth when it comes to "what I need to do" about my spouse or children. Some will tell you what to do because it benefits them. Their counsel isn't in your best interest or your family's. We must not let our parents overstep their boundaries in our homes, either. It's not good to have them over-involved in the home of a married couple. I've seen homes dominated by someone's parent, and they're often full of strife, discontent and misery. Some parents even try to control their children's home by withholding finances and gifts, or through the silent treatment if they don't do what they say. This is unbiblical and the spirit of Jezebel, which seeks to control and manipulate people. I have received, and still receive, good counsel from my parents. That's just what it is....counsel. I respect them more because they don't impose their wills on me. Please keep in mind that I make this next statement as a non-custodial parent. I believe that the non-custodial parent should be respected in decision-making concerning their children... to the extent of their involvement in their lives. If they aren't responsible for their children's emotional, social and financial wellness, why should they be involved deeply in decision-making? Some will argue that because they are biological parents they should have an equal say in your home no matter what they do. The truth is that, when we have children out of wedlock, we pay a price for that sin. Sometimes the price includes forgoing everyday decision-making in their lives. Good non-custodial parents' opinions and requests should be honored as much as possible. If they do their part, it's only fair to allow them the joy of being a part of their children's lives. I don't tell my son's mother what to do. I offer my advice and use words like, I would do. You should do... I would like... and... If you don't mind. I pray and do my best to foster a good relationship with her, so I can be a part of my son's life. Remember, I can't manage a house I don't live in.

You are going to have people tugging on you from all directions. What's important is that no one separates you as husband and wife. You must work to stay on one accord because satan is always trying to separate you. Your job is to submit to the will of God, not to your feelings, so you can do what is right despite what anyone else says. My wife and I make all decisions concerning our home, doing our best to follow the Holy Spirit's lead. We process all information, keeping the good and discarding the bad. At the end of the day, we're the ones who bear the responsibility of managing our home.

5

"MUTUAL RESPECT"

In a blended family, you and your spouse likely will be in contact with the other biological parent. Sometimes, it will be without both of you being present. If you're not mutually secure and respectful, things easily can take a turn for the worse.

It takes maturity to handle this relationship. We must honor our spouses at all times, respecting them in and out of their presence. Remember, satan is always looking for a way to trip us up, and one trip up can break up a happy family. The part of my wedding vows that always hits home is the part about forsaking all others. To forsake means to abandon, neglect, depart, leave or discard. Keep in mind that when you married your spouse, you should have closed the door on all other emotional attachments, including those with anyone you had a child with. Your spouse is your priority, and no one but God should be a higher priority. Your job is to make sure your spouse is comfortable with your relationship with the other parent. We must avoid doing things that sow seeds of distrust and jealousy in the minds of our spouses. If you can't talk to the other parent with your spouse in the room, there's a problem. Personal phone conversations with the other parent that aren't about children can cause problems. Meeting without your spouse or your spouse's knowledge to pick up the children will cause problems. Being over-attached to an ex's family could cause a problem. Likewise, inviting the other parent to your home without the approval or knowledge of your spouse can lead to problems. If you think that something is going to be a problem, you should examine it. It's better to be sure about your actions. That way you can avoid negative consequences.

You may not have any of these issues, but there are times where you'll have to go the extra mile to make sure your spouse feels secure. That means courtesy calls when you arrive at a destination and when you leave. You may have to avoid being over-affectionate to the other parent. I know that you're saying to yourself that you shouldn't have to do all of that. For a blended family to work, though, both of you will have to go the extra distance to honor your spouse. Don't let the other parent show disrespect toward your spouse. You should handle all inappropriate comments and actions immediately. Your spouse shouldn't have to ask you to address issues you can take care of yourself. If you ignore them, your spouse will feel that you approve of them, and a feeling of disrespect is sure to follow.

An issue surely to cause strife in a blended family is "insecurity." To avoid the effects of being insecure, a husband and wife must be secure in their relationship and with themselves. We must recognize that our spouses will have to interact with the other parents for the sake of the children. You being in the picture does not delete the other parent from the child's life. This is an opening for satan to try to fill your minds with all kinds of thoughts and emotions to make you jealous. For the sake of peace, we have to fight off these thoughts. If your spouse isn't acting in a way that would make you jealous, then the problem may be with you. Yes, you! You must learn how to adjust your attitude and trust your spouse. Where there are insecurities, trust is lacking. We can make things very uncomfortable by not trusting. From this come accusations and arguments that have no merit and don't have to happen. Let your spouse know that you trust him or her and that your spouse doesn't have to feel restricted when interacting with the other parent. Also, if you want to be trusted, show yourself to be trustworthy. Don't give your spouse something to be insecure about. Satan's job is to present opportunities for you to do something wrong. Your job is to respond in a way that pleases God. Remember, one mishap can cause years of uneasiness. It isn't worth it my friend. Reminiscing about your old relationship with the non-custodial parent is unacceptable. There's no need for you to talk about what used to be. You're not together for a reason, and you need to remind yourself of that when satan tries to lure you into that trap.

Before we say "I do," we should be clean of any soul ties to another person. What is a soul tie? A soul tie is a strong mental, emotional or physical connection to another person. It is usually established through emotional and physical bonding in a relationship. That's why God ordained sex only for married couples. He knew that this act would not be only a physical coming together but something that would affect us mentally and emotionally. When we have sex before marriage, we're forming a bond with someone without a covenant promise to us. If a strong bond is formed and the other leaves, our souls will long to reconnect with them. This is why some of us took different kinds of abuse. We have allowed ourselves to connect with someone who is not of God. This person has become a drug, and you long for a "fix," knowing that nothing good will come from being with the person. If you're having strong feelings for an ex or your child's parent, you could be suffering from a soul tie. The only person your soul should be connected to in that way is your spouse. The only way to be loosed from it is to not give yourself to that person by meditating on them, communicating with them or sleeping with them. You must pray to be free from all ungodly connections. You can do it! Whom the Son makes free is free indeed. (John 8:36) Decree and declare that you are free from all attachments to that person in Jesus' name. Speak liberty over yourself knowing that you can do all things through Christ who strengthens you. (Phil 4:13)

6

"NAME CALLING"

In my experience, this has to be one of the most controversial topics of blended families. What should a child call a non-biological parent? Do they call you Dad or Mom, or do they call you by your last name with the prefix Mr. or Mrs.? This can be very complicated. Let's explore some thoughts. First, we must never try to replace a biological parent. Many parents try to do this when they have had a bad relationship or when a biological parent refuses to take part in a child's life. Some parents try to make their child forget about their biological parent and accept the new spouse as a replacement. This is wrong. If we do this, we are likely going to have problems with our children. How many times have we heard of adult children searching for a long-lost parent? How many reunions have we watched on television or heard about where a child and parent reunite with joy, in spite of that parent's absence in the child's life. Often, the son or daughter forgives the parent's irresponsible acts just to have a relationship. Why is that? There will always be something in a child that longs to bond with biological parents. We can't replace or even suppress it. Children may not show this when young, but as they grow older, this longing can increase. If a biological parent chooses not to participate in the child's life that is the parent's loss. We should not keep children from their biological parent for our own selfish reasons. Neither should we lie to our children about the identity of their biological parent because of our shame and insecurities. We don't want to have that meeting with our child that begins with the question, why didn't you tell me?

Children will always long to know who had a part in shaping their DNA. We shouldn't deny them the right to find their identity. The non-biological parents should accept their role in the child's life without trying to be a replacement.

Parents also should not speak of the other parents in a negative way in the presence of children. This is easier said than done. Many of us have many unpleasant memories about the other parent. Some memories even may be fresh on your hearts. There's a reason that you two aren't together, and some of you think your children should know why. We should resist the temptation to tell them. Even if it's true, please don't insult the other parent. Let children form their own opinions without your bias. When you insult their parent in their presence, you'll do two things. You'll fill children with bitterness that could produce unforgiveness, or you'll push them further away from you if they really love that parent. We should always be careful to do unto others as we would have them do unto us. You're the adult. Act like one.

If you find yourself continuing to insult the other parent, you're operating in unforgiveness yourself. That unforgiveness will manifest as bitterness and resentment in your spirit. Remember what our Lord says in the model prayer in Mathew 6:14-15. If we forgive men their trespasses, our Father in heaven will forgive us our trespasses. But if we don't forgive others, neither will we be forgiven. If you struggle with not being able to forgive, ask the Father to heal your heart. It helps to say to yourself that you forgive the person who upset you. The words will have power and can deliver you.

At the beginning of our marriage, our daughter asked me a question that I didn't know how to answer. At the dinner table one afternoon, she said, "Can we call you Daddy?" My heart warmed immediately. The children had been calling me by my first name every since I started dating their mom, but our relationship was changing. I had now been in their lives for two years. Surely, I loved them as a father. I went on field trips and doctor visits. I read them stories and played with them. We went to church. I bought their mom a car so that they could get around. They were even covered by my medical insurance before we married. I had supplied their needs and was there for them in every way for some time now. I had been doing the job but hadn't taken on the title. My wife and I talked about it and decided that it was okay. Two factors came into play, the nature of our relationship and their age. First, the question of calling someone Mom or Dad shouldn't be considered unless you're married. Marriage signifies commitment. Your children shouldn't call someone Mom or Dad who hasn't committed in the sight of God to the family. What would happen if it didn't work out? Would the next person you are in a relationship with be their mom or dad, too? Their age also should be considered. A thirteen-year-old may not be as comfortable as a 4-year old calling your spouse Dad when he has a healthy relationship with his biological father. I came into my children's lives when they were 3 and 4. This made the transition a lot easier. Being married to the child's parent does not necessarily entitle us to being called Mom or Dad.

Here's why. Children must feel that you genuinely love them. They have to see and feel love by what you say and do. They must know that you treat them the same as your own children. If you don't love them, they can tell, and they won't form a connection with you. Forming a connection with you is important because it isn't a birth connection like they have with their biological parents. If there's no connection, they won't want to call you Mom or Dad. If they're forced to do it, they'll hate it and you. Be sure to talk about these issues as a family and let God lead you. Some biological parents will detest that their children call someone else Mom or Dad. There's no need for this if they're secure in their relationship with their children. Usually, these feelings are insecurities coming to the surface.

Good parents aren't threatened by someone else because they're doing their job as parents and the child does know who the biological mom or dad is. Keep in mind that I write this as a non- custodial parent. There could be the chance my son will call someone else Dad. I'm okay with this. I have to be. It's something you have to deal with when you have children out of wedlock.   If you marry into a family with older children, their addressing you as Mom or Dad may take time, or it may not happen at all. That family, however, should find a way to make sure the non-biological parent is addressed respectfully.

You're not my mother [or father]! Many non-biological parents hear this. It has great potential for hurt feelings if you let it. We hear it mostly when disciplining a child. We also hear it when we begin trying to connect with them. Children will view you as a plus as long as you're buying things for them or treating them to things. You can become the enemy, however, the minute you try to discipline. Satan wants to use their words and actions to cause your heart to be hardened toward them. If your heart hardens, you will never connect with them. If you don't connect with them, it is likely to cause issues within your family. Do you see where this is going? How do you know you heart is hardening? Your heart is being hardened when you stop caring. Your heart is hardening when you give up on trying to connect. Satan loves to divide and conquer, and, yes, he will use children if he can. The key to shielding your heart from hurt is to understand that children are immature and naïve, and, most of the time, don't know what's right or wrong. You're the adult and must never stop loving them despite their immaturity. They know words will hurt and use them to get their way. You must take on the attitude of Jesus on the cross. "Forgive them Father for they know not what they do." (Luke 23:34) Often, they won't appreciate the sacrifices you make for them. Prayerfully, as they grow up, they will realize how blessed they are to have you in their lives and will thank God for you.

The one thing that most non-custodial parents are concerned about is the treatment of their child. We pray to God to watch over our children while they are not in our immediate presence. You should consider yourself favored by God if you are a non-custodial parent and your child lives in a home full of love and support. You should do your best to work with that family and honor the structure set in that home. I would count it as a blessing from God that my child is in a good home with someone who would not hurt him. For that, I would pocket my pride and have no problem with someone else being called Mom or Dad because he or she is truly helping me. There should be no problems as long as they love your child just as much as you and aren't trying to replace you. A spouse being called Mom or Dad does not strip the non-custodial parent of parental rights and duties. It does show honor and respect to that spouse for his or her place in the child's life.

7

"PARENTING FROM THE OUTSIDE"

On March 7, 2005 my wife and I closed on our first home in Summerville, South Carolina. We were originally from North Charleston and, to say we were excited about moving would be an understatement. We looked forward to all the new things that come with moving. We would be in a new township with opportunities to meet new people and experience new things. I was more excited, however, about something else. Where we were moving was a ten-minute drive from where our son lived. We could now be more a part of his life and he more of ours. If he ever needed us, we would just be around the corner. It would also be easy to pick him up to spend the night or to go anywhere we were going. We could be actively involved in his school and attend any of its events. Life was good. One day on the way from church, we wanted to pick him up to spend the rest of the afternoon with us. I called his home a few times but got no answer.   In my spirit, I felt something was not right. We decided to drop by to see if everything was okay. What happened next was one of the major disappointments in my life. We arrived at the house to see a car being packed to leave. I asked his mother what was going on. She told me that they were moving to Georgia. The worst of the story is that we could not even say goodbye to our son. She had already taken him away and had just come back to get the rest of her things. I had no idea they were moving. All of this happened less than a month of our settling in the area. Now, not only did he not live in our house, he lived five hours away in another state. How could I be the father I wanted to be for him from such a distance?

If you're a non-custodial parent, you must make every effort to be a part of your children's lives and assure them that they're a part of yours. Neither distance nor the circumstances of life are excuses for not being a responsible parent. 1 Tim 5:8 says that"...if a man provide not for his own, he hath denied the faith and is worse than an unbeliever." We cannot make excuses about what we can't do. However, we can have a determination to have a good relationship with our children. You might have to go the extra mile to show your children that you love them. You can't settle into the mindset that they love you just for being a sperm or an egg donor. Love is an action verb that must be demonstrated. In some cases, the custodial parent may be misleading the child about your feelings towards them. If you're never around, this would be easy to believe, but don't give the enemy that kind of ammunition. Forget all the excuses about what you can't do and be responsible. Do everything that you can to show your children you love them and want to be in their lives. Don't let work or your current relationship keep you from being a parent.

Communication- Technology has provided us with many different ways to communicate with one another. We can text, email, video chat or connect via social networks. These vehicles of communication are not limited by distance and are great ways to keep connected to those we love. An email or text won't show your true emotion, and the reader will have to decipher the true sentiment of your words. Some communication media keep you connected, yet they are impersonal. Using video chat takes it a step above by allowing your child to hear and see you.   Hearing an actual voice and seeing you are far more comforting than reading words. Even through video, your presence can soothe and reassure children of your love. Also, never underestimate the power of the telephone. It says that I was thinking of you, in spite of what I'm doing, and made time for you. It's simple, quick and effective.

Quality Time- Nothing can replace time spent with your child. We may have to put in time, effort and money to plan the time, but it's necessary. It takes time together to form the bond that parent and child needs. Some of us may be upset that our children are not as close to us as we would like. Ask yourself these questions. How much time have I spent with them? Are they priorities in my life, or do I make them optional? Do I keep my promises to them? Do I constantly tell them I love them and show it by my actions? The answer to these questions may cause you to make some changes. Many of us use the excuse that we're not in position to do certain things for our child. Ask yourself this. If you had custody, would it be optional or would you have to make provisions? Your children should never feel like outsiders when they visit you. If you have children who live with you, make sure you're not treating them better than the other child that is visiting. They may have different things because they live with you, but your love for all should be the same. When we plan our family vacations, we plan for our son to go, too. We don't want him to feel left out when he hears about the fun we had. We also take as many pictures as we can. That way, when we view the slideshow of our lives, he knows he's a part of our family. Also, pictures are a good way to refute a custodial parents attempt to influence your children in a negative way. When your children grow up, they can always look back and remember the events associated with a picture. If a custodial parent tells your child that you love your spouse or other children more, the moments you capture on camera will say otherwise.

Child Support-Paying child support doesn't exempt you from providing other things for your children. I'm sure that many of you are upset and bitter over this issue, but your children don't understand that. They won't see your love in the child support you send but through the things you do. They won't understand that money is being garnished from your paycheck for them or that you had to provide medical care. What they will notice is that you didn't give them anything for their birthday. They will notice that there was no gift from you under the Christmas tree. They will notice that you didn't even buy them a box of pencils for school. Don't let anger and bitterness stop you from doing the best you can for your child. My wife and I make sure that we send something in the mail that our son can open on holidays and special occasions. The gift says that we took time to show him our love, no matter how small or big it is. It says that we want to take the time to show him how important he is to us.

Like most parents, I want my children to respect me. We get a certain amount of respect for having the title of father and mother. The rest of that respect will be earned by the love you demonstrated toward them. Even though our son lives hours away, we do as much as we can to show him that love. My father didn't live with us, but he was very much a part of mine and my brother's lives. We had his phone number. We knew where he lived and spent nights there. He visited us. He also liked to take us to a place called Cruisers for hamburgers. His presence in my life was the main reason I stayed out of trouble. As a non-custodial parent, you may not be able to do all the things you want, but your presence can benefit your children. It is sad to think that many good parents aren't allowed to be a part of their child's life. This is amazing since there are so many deadbeat parents who could care less about their children. You and the custodial parent might have unresolved issues. You might be separated by distance. Someone may even be denying you the right to spend time with your child.   Don't let that stop you from being who you are supposed to be to your child. Decide today to abandon all excuses why you can't do something and trust God to give you strength and wisdom to be a great parent. Pray and trust God to move the heart of the non-custodial parent who is making things difficult for you. If you are a custodial parent denying a parent access into a child's life for no good reason, I pray that the Holy Spirit convicts you to change. Every child deserves to spend time with a caring parent. Remember, it's not about either parent, but what's in the best interest of your child.

8

"HOLIDAY SHUFFLE"

Where and with whom will we spend this holiday?
The question can be the cause of much confusion in
your family. There are factors to consider. Are we
going to visit the wife's family or the husband's? Will
you keep the children with you or allow them to
separate to be with some of their other family
members?   Do we just want to stay at home this
holiday? Grandparents will always want to see their
grandchildren, and your parents will always want to
see you. What do you do when your child's

grandparent is not your parent? Are we confused yet?

There's a lot that goes into planning a holiday in a blended family. I will tell you right now that I don't have an iron-clad solution. I would like to offer some pointers that can guide you in the direction of making the best decision for your family.

First, we must consider the frequency and amount of time we spend with a certain family group. In many marriages, one spouse typically spends more time with the family of the other spouse than with his or her own family. This may be because of distance, or it could just be circumstantial. Eventually, spouses will want to make time to be with their family members, too. We must be careful not to become complacent or selfish if our spouses spend more time with our family than they do with theirs. There will be times where they'll want to be with their family, and we must understand their feelings. We have to learn how to balance out holiday time and make compromises for the greater good. For a few years, we tried to visit all of our family members on the holidays. We would start early and go to the nearest house first as we navigated through our city. After several hours and much gasoline, we decided that it wasn't worth it driving all over the place trying to please everyone. We decided that we would stay home on some holidays and alternate visiting families on other holidays.

We also considered the ages of our children. When they were young, they simply went wherever we went. Things, however, change as they get older. Here's an example. Let's say that we are spending Thanksgiving this year with my mother, who isn't their biological grandmother. Their biological father is having Thanksgiving at his house this year. His entire family will be there, including the biological brothers and sisters of our children. They are now teenagers and have expressed an interest in visiting their father. Just because my wife and I are going to my mother's doesn't mean that the children have to come with us. They're older now and deserve an opportunity to spend some holidays with their biological family. I know that we don't like to separate our families, but at times this may be in the best interest of all involved.

Be careful to avoid being selfish with your children on the holidays. If you and the child's parent have a good relationship, you can work out a reasonable agreement. Alternating who will have the children on holidays is good. If I have the children on Christmas this year, then I can expect not to have them on next year, but I'll have them on Thanksgiving. This is only fair if the non-custodial parent wants to be a part of the child's life. Sadly, many parents won't face this dilemma. Too many non-custodial parents just don't care. I guess you have to look at the bright side... more time with your child.

9

"DISCIPLINE"

Society has gone a long way in proving that the lack of discipline leads to chaos. Detention centers can't be built fast enough to house the growing population of young lawbreakers. Our school systems are becoming worse because of unruly students. Executing and receiving discipline is not debatable. Proverbs 13: 24 says, "Whoever spares their rod hates their children, but the one who loves their children is careful to discipline them." My mother must have really loved us. There was no rod sparing in our house. It was a great deterrent from being disrespectful in class. The neighbors could discipline you if they caught you doing something wrong. Then they would bring you home, and your parents would discipline you again. These days, we don't allow anyone to discipline our children. I can understand this, given the terrible state of our society. Some parents, however, won't even allow others to orally correct their children even when they are obviously disrespectful.   It's a shame when no one can say anything about your child, especially when you know that your child is no angel. Parents and teachers used to work together. Now, parents believe little, lying Johnny over the teacher. This shows the child that he doesn't have to respect the authority of the teacher because you don't. Maybe that's why they grow up not respecting anyone in authority, including a supervisor or law enforcement officer. It's just a thought. Scripture does indicate that discipline should be done carefully. We should make sure that we are not abusing our children. We shouldn't discipline when we are angry. We should also let them know why they are receiving discipline. Disciplining them just because you can is abuse.

"Discipline your son while there is hope, but do not [indulge your angry resentments by undue chastisements and] set yourself to his ruin." (Proverbs 19:18 Amp) As our children get older, our methods of discipline may change, but we should not stop it all together. I believe not to discipline your child is a form of neglect. When we don't discipline them we reject our biblical duties. A lack of discipline will also teach a child that there is no consequence for their wrong actions.   Disciplining your children can save their lives. Here's my point. Law enforcement never had to correct me because of all the discipline I received from my mother.   Some of us wait too long to start disciplining our children. I have seen the regretful tears of parents who allowed their children to do as they pleased at a young age and then tried to discipline them when they were older. To discipline your children is Godly. Don't wait until it's too late. You could be saving their lives.

Okay. We've established that we should discipline our children. But how does it work in a blended family? The biological parent automatically has this right, but what about the non-biological parent? Many will be critical of a non-biological parent disciplining their child, grandchild, niece or nephew. How in the world do we handle this? First, we must revisit a key point from Chapter 4. *A person does not have the right to manage a household that he or she does not live in.* Unbiased advice from trusted loved ones should be considered, but all decisions concerning the operation of your home should be made by you and your spouse. The only qualification in considering whether or not a non-biological parent disciplines a child is love. Does the non-biological parent love your child as they would their own? Is there a difference in how they treat their biological children and yours? A non-biological parent who shows unconditional love for non-biological children should be allowed to discipline them. If non-biological parents aren't allowed this right, they will not be respected by the child. The main resistance, if any, you'll get will be from the non-custodial parent or other family members. These will be the people who want you to treat the children just like your own except when it comes to discipline. They want you to make sure the children have a roof over their head, working utilities, food on the table, clothes on their back and medical insurance and to see that all of their needs are met. They don't want you, however, to discipline them. That is hypocritical and unreasonable. The non-biological parents' unconditional love for the children will show that they won't abuse them. If a non-biological parent is not allowed to discipline, it will diminish his or her authority in the house and cause division within the home. The children will feel that they don't have to listen and can constantly create friction between husband and wife. The biological parent will be defensive, and the non-biological parent will feel disrespected. If these issues aren't resolved, it could end in bitterness and divorce.

Non-custodial, biological parents should be informed if their child is being disciplined by a non-biological parent. If they have concerns, they should be allowed to express them. All parties involved should work together to reach an understanding of what is acceptable. While you might not agree on all the issues, open communication is a must.

10

"LETTING GO"

As custodial parents, one of the harshest realities we can experience is hearing those dreadful words, "I want to go live with my mom or dad." Can you picture Homer Simpson choking little Bart Simpson and saying, "Why you little...." I'm sure that's how many of us have felt, or will feel, when faced with this. We may use adjectives such as ungrateful, unappreciative, uncaring, selfish, foolish, rude, simple and thoughtless to describe our kids at that time. Usually, you would have made all the sacrifices you could so that they have the best life possible. Now they have the audacity to want to leave the covering of your home and connect with the noncustodial parent. Are you serious? Yes, I am! This is one possibility you can face in a blended family. Of course, there are times when children say this just because they don't like the discipline they're getting at home. There may come a time, though, when they mean it. I believe there are three reasons a child wants to leave the familiarity of home to live with a non-custodial parent. Let's look at them.

Emotional Bonding-The first reason has to do with satisfying the desire they have to be close to their other parent. Remember what I told you earlier. There will always be something in a child that wants to connect with a biological parent. The magnet of their soul will have a strong pull for its earthly source. Knowing that parent can give children insight on why they are the way they are. This will allow our children to better understand themselves. I mentioned at the beginning of this book how I went to live with my father for a season. Living with him helped me understand myself. He was able to show me what was in me and who I could be. I look like him. I walk and stand just like he does. I have most of the same mannerisms. We also have the same sense of humor.

The light bulb went on in my head. This is why I am the way I am. I get it from my father's DNA. Of course, I also have similarities with my mother. She is a great encourager and people person. Knowing both of my parents helped me to understand the whole me. Maybe that's why some children have wandering minds and feel incomplete. When you don't know your parents, it's hard to know and understand yourself. Whether that parent is good or bad, your child will want to find out. It may be necessary to allow children time with the other parent so that they can see what is engrafted inside their selves. This will give them insight to improve on the great things, or recognize at an early age the bad habits they need to defeat to be successful. For this cause, you may need to let your child go for a season or even indefinitely.

Greener Grass- Your children may want to leave home because they believe things will be better with the non-custodial parent. They may enjoy one good weekend or summer and equate that to permanently living with that parent. They may feel that they can get away with more mischief and have things their way away from home. They might not like discipline, but we are biblically instructed to give it to them.

They may just look at superficial things like cars, homes, clothes, etc. One parent may have amassed more things, but that doesn't qualify him or her to be a good parent. Showering children with money and gifts is not a substitute for the love, structure and support they need. Things can't speak life into or give direction and structure to a child. A video game system, computer, cell phone and other electronic gadgets may keep them entertained, but none can show children love or offer heartfelt advice on how to handle a situation at school. A child's emotional, social and physical well-being must be accounted for at all times. Cars break down and everything can be lost in a natural disaster, but real love is something that can never be taken away. The saying is so true. The grass is not always greener on the other side of the fence. What appears to be may not be the reality of a situation. It's up to us to show children in an unbiased way that the greener grass they see may be an illusion. Allowing them to cross the fence could be detrimental to their lives. If the grass truly is greener that should not be the sole reason for your child wanting to leave home. We must not allow our children to be shallow decision-makers. Depending on their age and maturity level, there may be an upside to allowing them to cross the fence into so-called greener pastures. Sometimes, it could be beneficial to give them what they want, so they can see for themselves that it's not what they thought it would be. This could give them a greater appreciation of what you have provided for them. After all, Dorothy said, "There's no place like home."

Better Environment-Finally, your child may genuinely want to be in a better environment. A home without peace and love is a frustrating environment to grow up in. Before you get upset at your child, consider the atmosphere around you. Is there constant confusion at your home? Are there illegal activities in your home or neighborhood that threaten the safety of your child? Is your home suitable to live in? Do your utilities frequently get interrupted? How stable is your relationship? Are the emotional, social and physical needs of your child being provided for? Is your child free to express opinions in a respectful way? Are you so engulfed with your spouse that you have forgotten to be a mother or father to your child? Do these things cause your child to act out in school? These are just a few of the many questions we should ask ourselves. If the other parent can provide a safer and more stable environment for your child to dwell, you may need to let your child leave. If you really love your child, his or her best interest should be your main concern. You can't let your ego, pride or shame stop you from doing what is best for the child. Child support should not be an issue. Parents should position themselves financially so that child support is not the bulk of their income. If your house can't operate without child support, you're in trouble. Child support is ordered to help the custodial parent take care of the needs of that child and not to totally support the custodial parent. Sad to say, many parents won't allow their child to have a better opportunity because they rely primarily on child support to support their home. Think about it. You are literally selling your child's life for money. That makes you a pimp!

How in the world do we deal with this? First, we must learn not to take it personally. Their desire to live with the other parent may not be a reflection of the job you're doing rearing them. Many parents will take this as a personal insult, rather than seeing it for what it is. Remember that children can be simple and naïve. They lack the vision and ability to access the whole situation. It is unlikely that they could be filled with compassion to consider yours or anyone else's feelings about the matter. They just see what they see and want what they want. You must be careful to not become bitter and feel insulted by their request.

If you become offended, it will put up a wall of separation between you and them that will sever the lines of communication. Accept it for what it is. Naïve children will make thoughtless and emotional requests. Many are invalid and some will have validity. There is no defined answer on when to let your child live with the other parent, or even if you should. To sort it out, we should rely on the wisdom from Proverbs 3:5-6. "Trust in the Lord with all thine heart; and lean not to thine own understanding. In all thy ways acknowledge Him, and He shall direct thy paths." There may come a time in your life where letting go will be in the best interest of the child. It will be painful. It will require adjusting. Most of all, it will require prayer. Let God know that you trust Him and ask Him to give you clear direction on this matter. To trust Him, you must know Him and have fellowship with Him. Be sure you have peace in your spirit from God that you are making the right decision. I'm not saying that it will be an easy decision, but it should be a God-decision. We should understand that His ways are higher than our ways and His thoughts are higher than our thoughts. (Isaiah 55:9) He knows the beginning from the end and has already made everything right.   "And we know that all things work together for good to them that love God, to them who are called according to his purpose." Romans 8:28

What the Non-Custodial Parent Should Consider

A non-custodial parent who wants to remove a child should consider a few things. I use the word "remove," considering there is not a need for the child to live with the non-custodial parent. The most important detail is your reason for wanting the child. Are your motives pure, or is there an agenda behind your wanting your child? Are you trying to hurt the other parent? Are you trying to prove something to someone else? Are you trying to exploit your children for gifts and talents they have or a service they can render for you?   Does the child even want to live with you? The only reason for thinking of removing your child from a stable environment should be to provide better opportunities that will not have a negative effect on their emotional, social or physical well-being.   A non-custodial parent should not want the child for the sole reason of not paying child support. That is selfish and shows that that parent will be inclined to put his or her needs before the best interest of the child. The cost of taking care of that child or children should be evaluated. It may be more than you can handle or the child support you are paying. Medical care and schooling should be considered. Children grow and will constantly need new clothes. Your grocery and utility bills will increase. Are you able to provide for them in an equal or better way than their current environment? If not, they could despise you for taking them away from what is normal. Are you breaking up a home for selfish reasons? Your child may have siblings and friends they're deeply connected to, and pulling them away can cause them to have withdrawals from home. Is that child the oldest and is he or she protective of the family? Will taking your child away from the custodial parent cause tension and resentment between your child and you? Is this a good age to remove your child? How will your child's coming to live with you affect your current family or job situation? Will your spouse love your child like his or her own? Do you have time to spend with your child that will allow you to bond? Non-custodial parents must also make sure they are trusting God to make this decision. You must make sure that removing your child is not for selfish reasons or to please others. It should be a God-decision that will help and not hurt your child.

CONCLUSION

Wow! This is definitely a lot of information. Did you think being a part of a blended family would require so much work? Most of us didn't. Some of you are saying, "I didn't sign up for this." Yes, you did! You just forgot to read the fine print in the blended family contract. We should resolve in our hearts to make our families work. It will require great effort to avoid failure. To be successful at anything in life will require hard work. Your blended family can work! You can overcome the obstacles in its way. The key to a successful blended family is for a husband and wife to work together to agree on the issues you face. The more you're in agreement, the less room there is for strife to creep in and cause further division and confusion in your marriage. Both of you must resist being selfish and work for the greater good of your family. This book is a reference to help you get on track. It will help guide and referee you to being victorious in your family life. It won't, however, substitute for communication between husband and wife. Let it be a guide as you talk about the issues in your family. Open-minded communication will play a crucial role in maintaining family order. It is my prayer that you find peace and order by reading this book.

Typically, blended families are connected to other blended families. Let us make sure that we make a conscious effort to help one another. Someone you know is waiting for this life-changing information. Please recommend or buy this book for those you know will benefit from it. In doing so, you could save a marriage and change lives.